LINCOLNSHIRE

THE PHOTOGRAPHIC COLLECTION

The compilation of these two books is dedicated to Patricia Ranby whose fun and frivolity shaped our young lives.

LINCOLNSHIRE

THE PHOTOGRAPHIC COLLECTION

DAVID CUPPLEDITCH

SUTTON PUBLISHING

This edition first published in 2003 by
Sutton Publishing Limited · Phoenix Mill
Thrupp · Stroud · Gloucestershire · GL5 2BU

The Lincolnshire Coast was first published in 1996 by Sutton Publishing Limited
The Lincolnshire Wolds was first published in 1997 by Sutton Publishing Limited

British Library Cataloguing in Publication Data
A catalogue record for this book is available from the British Library.

ISBN 0 7509 3352 6

Typeset in 10/12pt Perpetua.
Typesetting and origination by
Sutton Publishing Limited.
Printed and bound in Great Britain by
J.H. Haynes & Co. Ltd, Sparkford.

CONTENTS

Part One

Part Two

Part One
The Lincolnshire Coast

Mablethorpe floods, 1953. On hand to dole out tea to emergency helpers who cleaned up the mess is this group of volunteers. The ambulance is standing by, but the most important vehicle is the NAAFI wagon!

All along this coast many sailors and swimmers have been thankful for the lifeboats. This is the *Heywood*, presented by Mr Heywood Lonsdale in 1883 and stationed in Mablethorpe.

A fishing tournament at Boston, *c.* 1910.

INTRODUCTION

The Lincolnshire coast is one of the few places left in Britain where there is a peaceful feeling of solitude. Because of its open spaces this shoreline makes an ideal venue for anyone wanting to escape the hustle and bustle of modern day life and 'recharge their batteries'. There is mile upon mile of lonely salt-marsh, sand-dune and shrub only a stone's throw away from the busy resorts of Cleethorpes, Mablethorpe, Sutton and Skegness. Here there is room to breathe, there is serenity, and it is often bracing!

The writer of a travel book published in Edwardian times summed it up when he said;

> The characteristics of the coast scenery of Skegness, Sutton-on-Sea and Mablethorpe are so similar that a description of one would serve for the other two. In each place there is a magnificent stretch of clean and firm sands, with a line of sandhills stretching on and on for miles in either direction between the shore and the bordering farm-lands. These hillocks, clothed in part by grass and plants, afford cosy resting nooks and shelters from sun or wind, and are scarcely inferior to the sands themselves as an attraction to visitors.

Many years later, D.H. Lawrence visited this coastline on holiday and indeed many Lincolnshire place-names can be found in his novels.

The area has also played host to royalty. HRH Princess Anne visited the East Coast on 15 September 1993, when she opened the new primary school at North Somercotes. She also visited the Willoughby Group of Riding for the Disabled near Alford, and fitted in a trip to Theddlethorpe on that same busy morning. Just as the old HRH Duchess of Gloucester and HRH Duke of Edinburgh were quick to visit the 1953 Great Flood.

Historically this coastline has been a combination of floods, sea defences, erosion, reclamation, smugglers and shipwrecks. Five medieval churches have been swallowed up by the sea and the flood of 1571 prompted Jean Ingelow to pen her famous poem 'The High Tide on the Coast of Lincolnshire'. In 1953 a total of 233 people died as a result of the Great East Coast Flood, thirty-five of whom died in Mablethorpe and Sutton. But the most notable reminder of the past lies in Fishtoft where the roadsign points to

'SCALP' and 'CUT END'. Down this road on the bank of The Haven lies Pilgrims' Pillar (erected in 1957) as Fishtoft's memorial to the Pilgrim Fathers.

It was from here that a group of Separatists first set sail in 1607. They were betrayed by their ship's captain, arrested and brought back to Boston in open boats where they were ridiculed as a 'spectacle and a wonder to the multitude'. They evetually fled to Holland and formed part of the group known as the Pilgrim Fathers, who sailed in the *Mayflower* from Plymouth to New England in 1620. A total of thirteen vessels were chartered to carry the Puritans (as they had become known) across the Atlantic, including the *Arabella*, named after Lady Arabella, the wife of Isaac Johnston of Boston.

From Frieston shore to Wainfleet Sand there are dangerous mud flats from where the terms 'fen-slodger' and 'gozzard' originate. But from Gibraltar Point to Cleethorpes there is an almost uninterrupted stretch of fine golden sand. In the Great Exhibition of the 1920s, tons of Mablethorpe sand were transported to Wembley for use in displays. Nor is this coastline devoid of vegetation. The Victorian delicacy samphire, which Mrs Beeton used to pickle, grows in abundance.

At one time the Lincolnshire coast was well known for oysters and shellfish. And indeed my earliest memory of a visit to Anderby Creek in the fifties digging for cockles is imprinted on my mind forever. It was autumn, I was cold and hypothermia nearly set in. The typhoid epidemic at the turn of the century killed off the old oyster trade, while pollution in the North Sea has done much damage to shrimping and lobster fishing. Despite this heavy pollution, grey seals still return to Donna Nook every year in late November/early December to give birth to their pups. The dunes are covered with mothers and their young while the fathers or large bulls wait close by.

Many famous people in the field of entertainment have been born along this coast. Arthur Lucan (better known as 'Ole Mother Riley') was born in Sibsey, near Boston, Elizabeth Allan, the Hollywood actress, was born in Skegness, and the late Patrick Wymark and Patricia Hodge count themselves as 'Meggies'. Numerous stars and personalities have appeared, both at the Embassy and at Cleethorpes pier, fulfilling the role which the Clements carried out for a number of years.

Everyone has their own memories of sea-side holidays, whether it be ice-cream, donkey rides or penny slot machines. Some of us can look back with nostalgia at those days, where the smell of ozone intermingled with the smell of fish and chips and vinegar! The sound of children's laughter was only interrupted by waves or squawking gulls circling overhead. Ultimately you recall the freedom far removed from road rage, stress and the Heath Robinson bureaucracy we all live with today, and you think 'Ah, those were the days'.

David Cuppleditch
1996

BOSTON

One of the four rivers which run into the Wash is the Witham. This waterway which joins Boston with Lincoln has been responsible for providing countless hours of fun to both professional and amateur seafarers.

Boston, or Botolphstown, is the start of this journey along the Lincolnshire coast. In this photograph of boats on the Witham, the paddle steamer SS *Privateer* is acting as a tug to one of the sailing craft leaving Boston port.

It is difficult to believe that in Norman and medieval times Boston's port was one of the chief commercial ports in England, trading with ports in Northern Europe, Flanders and the Rhineland.

When Boston Dock was enlarged in 1882, at a cost of £170,000, the Mayor and his wife, Mr and Mrs J. Simmonds, cut the first sod. Looking on, with plans rolled up, is William Wheeler, Borough Surveyor.

Three mills used to stand on what is now the centre of Boston Dock. These are two of them. But all along the Lincolnshire coast lies a graveyard of this once flourishing trade.

Of the few remaining mills, and one in working order, is the Maud Foster Mill erected for Thomas and Isaac Reckitt in 1819. The name of Reckitt is retained in the successful company of Reckitt & Colman.

The familiar and distinctive features of the paddle tug SS *Privateer*, which travelled all around the Wash taking parties of people from Skegness pier to places as far away as Hunstanton. This photograph was taken at Packhorse Quay.

When John Rennie's Boston bridge was pulled down in April 1913 the SS *Privateer* was called upon to help demolish it. Sadly this friendly little tug was sunk in 1914 in the first days of the First World War while towing off France. John Rennie achieved wider fame as the designer of Waterloo Bridge in London.

This was how Boston Dock looked at the turn of the twentieth century, when timber was the major import from Scandinavia.

And this is how it looked in the '50s, still importing timber!

An earlier vicar was A.M. Cook (1931–46) who wrote his short history of Boston; this became so popular that it was reprinted in 1948. Later Cook became Sub-Dean of Lincoln Cathedral (1946–61).

Of course the familiar landmark all around Boston is the Stump, which has acted as a beacon to many ships.

Here we see a section of Boston United's devoted fans. Photographed on the 18 December 1970 at their game with York City.

Just in front of the Stump in the Market Place is a statue of Herbert Ingram, founder of the *Illustrated London News* who drowned in 1860 in a tragic accident on Lake Michigan with his eldest son.

The Guildhall in South Street (next to Fydell House and currently Boston museum) is the building in which some of the Pilgrim Fathers were imprisoned. Incidentally, the ivy has been removed from Fydell House because of the damage it caused to the brickwork and fabric of the building.

Since the days of the Pilgrim Fathers Boston has retained strong links with the USA. In 1630 seven ships sailed under the Revd Isaac Johnson with such a preponderance of Boston men that Massachusetts' capital was given the town's name. In 1633 the famous preaching vicar John Cotton went there, and also Richard Bellingham, who became governor of Massachusetts. Here we see the Cotton Chapel in St Botolph's Church.

In the 1920s Sir Francis Fox visited the Stump and expressed his concern about the state of the tower. It was not until 1927, when the roof began to show alarming signs of decay, that the architect Sir Charles Nicholson was asked to report on the building. His report sparked off the massive restoration to which Boston, Massachusetts, gave £11,000; this was presented on 8 July 1931. The Stump is shown here when work was in progress.

Of all the postcards produced, this composite probably provides the most comprehensive view of Boston.

The most prolific photographer in Boston in Victorian and Edwardian times was George Hackford of Church Close.

The market is still as busy today as it was in Victorian times. This photograph was taken in about 1894.

Bostonians would always rise to the event. The celebration of Queen Victoria's Golden Jubilee in 1887 was marked by the roasting of an ox in the market place.

One landmark often overlooked and now rather neglected is the Hussey Tower (near Skirbeck Road). Lord Hussey was executed in 1541 at Lincoln for his part in the Lincolnshire Rebellion of 1536.

The Quay has changed somewhat with all the development that has taken place in Boston in recent years.

The Danish schooner *Frida*, the last sailing vessel to leave Boston Dock.

If this coast is a graveyard of former windmills the other casualty has been the parish church. Once the centre of every village, many of these churches now lie redundant. This is Fishtoft Church.

Butterwick Church has a fourteenth-century pulpit.

But if the parish church is in decline, local pubs seem to be on the up. This is The Barley Mow, Friskney, which thrives to this day although the name changed to The Witch and Cauldron in 1995.

The nearby Angel Inn in Wrangle.

The popularity of hospitable drinking in public houses, especially in the south of the county, gave rise to the brewing family of Bateman's. They purchased Wainfleet All Saints' Mill and now use the windmill as their trademark. The weather vane on top of the mill carries the Bateman logo.

This was the original Salem Bridge Mill, Wainfleet, which was still operating as a mill until about 1920, shortly before the Bateman family bought it.

SKEGNESS

Skegness Pier which was opened in June 1881, was wrecked in January 1978 when two sections were completely washed away by violent storms. This was all that was left (seen here) until a fire gutted the remains on 27 October 1985.

Near Skegness is the popular nature reserve of Gibraltar Point, now run by the Lincolnshire and South Humberside Trust for Nature Conservation.

The Jolly Fisherman poster, which appeared in 1908, advertised Great Northern Railway day trips at a cost of 3*s* from King's Cross to Skegness. The character has become synonymous with the town.

It would be difficult to think of Skegness without thinking of the word 'bracing' and vice versa. Yet its creator John Hassall received little financial reward. He was paid twelve guineas for his Jolly Fisherman poster and died in difficult circumstances in 1948. Hassall, seen here in his other favourite guise of amateur thespian, was made a Freeman of the Town in 1936.

The problem with Hassall was that he was an artist with a sense of humour, as can be seen in this follow-up poster stating: 'For all the ills we have to bear, There's nothing cures like East Coast air. It is SO bracing.'

The other man who did so much to put Skegness on the map was Billy Butlin, seen here in 1937 outside his holiday camp. It was Butlin who persuaded John Hassall to visit Skegness in 1936.

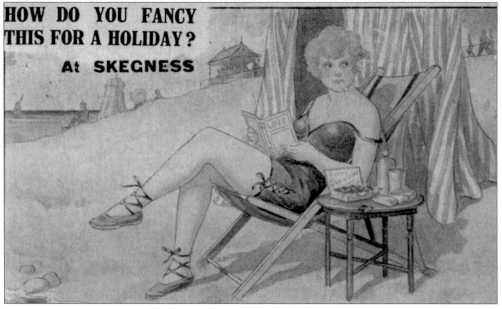

The postcard market flourished in the Edwardian era. Scantily clad mademoiselles enticed lustful young men on to the beach in the hope of catching a glance of ankle, or perhaps a bit more? Cards like this were sent in their thousands and paved the way for the more risqué joke cards that still sell today.

The big advantage that Skegness had was that it owned its own pier. Built in 1881, with Australian Jarrah decking and stout ironwork by Head, Wrightson & Co. of Teesdale, it was to remain a popular feature until 1978 when high winds and gales blew two sections down and wrecked it.

Another amusement was the *Eliza*, a two-masted ship (on the right of this postcard), which was beached and used as a museum.

Many families enjoyed having their photograph taken on the pier. This was the Hall Family from Louth. Just visible in the background is the makeshift diving board that 'Pegleg Gadsby' used to dive off for entertainment.

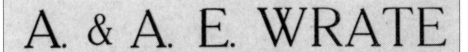

Capturing everything on camera was Wrate, the Skegness photographer whose studio was at 17 Lumley Road. It has often puzzled me why no one has ever compiled a dictionary of Lincolnshire photographers. Those who specialised in seaside scenes included Nainby of Alford, Bundock of Spilsby and Camm of Mablethorpe.

Charabanc parties flocked into Skegness for day trips.

Charabanc parked in front of the clock tower. Pevsner described the Jubilee Clock Tower of 1899 as architecturally negligible with a Big Ben top.

But there was still plenty for the day-tripper, including The Rock Gardens . . .

. . . or the Boating Lake, opened in 1924, which was such a success that it was extended two years later.

The swimming pool was also popular. When it opened in 1928 the bathing pool, with its twin chutes and diving boards, was the biggest on the East Coast, and was known as the New Wonder Pool of the East Coast.

Then there were the sands, with plenty of windbreakers to counteract that bracing wind.

This would have been the view most day-trippers would have seen if they had arrived at Skegness by train, looking down Lumley Road with the Lion Hotel on the left and Barlows on the right.

At the end of Lumley Road, just beside the clock tower, Les Howe (the Louth photographer) and family arrive for a day on the beach. Curiously enough, this was one of Wrates' walking photographs; it shows Clements Theatre in the background.

This is the clock tower, with Clements Theatre clearly visible in the middle of the photo.

For the more discerning there were two golf clubs in Skegness. One was at the North End, and this was the club house, now the North Shore Hotel.

The other golf club was based at the Vine Hotel. Known for a time as Enderby's Hotel, it still enjoys a good reputation. Tennyson is reputed to have played skittles here.

Only a short distance away is Coronation Walk, named after Edward VII's coronation in 1901. Coronation Walk started in Drummond Road and ran on to Richmond Drive, linking up with the Vine Hotel at Vine Walk.

Skegness probably enjoyed its heyday in those mid-war years of the '20s and '30s. There was a walk along the pier or, for the more adventurous, boat trips from the end of the pier.

This was the entrance to the Piazza Bathing Pool (now the Embassy), with its bandstand where holidaymakers could sit and enjoy the sunshine in deckchairs while listening to military brass band melodies. (Ah! Those were the days before portable radios or, even worse, ghetto-blasters!)

One example of the many thousand of holiday snaps taken by by Wrate's Photographers. This one is of two small boys enjoying their holiday. David Bolland is the small boy on the right.

It must have been difficult for those pioneers who helped to put Skegness on the map, such as John Hassall or Billy Butlin, or even Skegness Corporation, to envisage this scene. Looking north towards Ingoldmells, there are row upon row of caravans clustered around Butlin's Fun Coast World holiday camp.

Hidden away off Church Road North and Lincoln Road is the delightful church of St Clement's.

Like so many towns and villages on this coast Skegness is the combination of a seaside resort mixed with a farming community. Even today there are no fewer than three working farms in Skegness, with one in the form of a museum – Church Farm Museum (off Church Road, and opened to the public in 1976). Within the museum grounds there is an example of an eighteenth-century mud and stud Lincolnshire labourer's cottage, which was removed from Witham and re-erected here in about 1980.

The labourer's cottage was based on this sort of dwelling, which once was so commonplace along this coast. Joseph Willey (the Louth photographer) took this photograph in the Alford/Bilsby area in about 1870.

This was the interior of the tea rooms in Chapel St Leonards. Many buildings along this coast look as if a nautical flavour had played some part in their origination. The reason for this was that many pieces of old wrecks or ship timbers plundered from beached craft went into their fabric.

At nearby Gunby Hall can be seen the style in which some families lived before the advent of the dreaded bungalow. Long the seat of the Massingberd family, Gunby Hall was handed over to the National Trust by Sir Archibald Montgomery Massingberd in 1944, when this photograph was taken. It is open to the public from April to September.

During the forties and fifties model boats and yachts provided countless hours of enjoyment to children and adults alike. This was the yachting pool, Skegness.

For the elderly or middle-aged there was a game of bowls on North Parade.

By the 1930s the Jolly Fisherman had become the symbol of Skegness. It was the town's lucky charm, and reproductions of the Falstaffian character appeared on postcards, ash-trays, pottery and petrol caps! Despite the connection between Skegness and its Jolly Fisherman, a flood of postcards produced in the late '40s and '50s appeared with cats proposing a different kind of symbol.

It was almost as if Skegness had become intoxicated with the Jolly Fisherman and decisions had been made through an alcoholic haze. Fortunately the cat fad did not last long, and Skegness reverted to its dear old Jolly Fisherman once more.

SUTTON-ON-SEA

Between Skegness and Sutton lies Anderby Creek, where this selection of individual homes has been built on the edge of the beach.

From Skegness to Mablethorpe the sea defences are constantly reviewed. This is part of the long-term Ham project, which involves building new defences and beach nourishment. The photo was taken at Mogg's Eye and shows dredgers in the background.

This sign shows how the revetment is added to existing sea defences that have reached the end of their life.

Sutton-on-Sea became so popular in Edwardian times that a travel writer was prompted to comment that 'it would not be surprising in the near future to see Sutton, as in Skegness, develop from a village into a town'. Here we see the promenade on the seafront, which stretched for a quarter of a mile when it was built in 1885.

The two principal hotels were the Bacchus (once known as the Jolly Bacchus) ...

… and the Beach Hotel (now demolished). It is just visible in the background of this 1956 photograph.

Close to the old railway station was St Clement's Church, built in 1818 to replace the old medieval church which had slipped into the sea. Inside there is a stained glass memorial window to Bishop Bompas, first Bishop of the Yukon, commemorating his time as curate of this church.

The steam tramway that operated from Alford to Sutton, stopping at Bilsby, Markby and Hannah. It ran successfully for five years (1884–9).

Sutton station. When Sutton station opened in 1887, it effectively killed off the old steam tramway.

MARKBY CHURCH.

THE ONLY CHURCH IN ENGLAND WITH A THATCHED ROOF.

The chief attraction at Markby was the church with its thatched roof. The original roof was tiled, but in 1672 a churchwarden laid claim to the tiles in exchange for thatching the roof.

In 1908 some railway carriage bungalows were erected in Furlong Road. They were intended as temporary holiday cottages but all these years later are still standing and still used.

This is Waveland, one of the remaining cottages.

Throughout the '20s and '30s Sutton remained a popular resort, especially with children. This is one of the Howe children, wearing his dad's boots!

Bathing costumes could be a bit risqué!

Fashions change. This group of girls on Sutton beach in the early '50s would not have been seen dead in culottes in the '60s, but they were back in fashion in the 1990s.

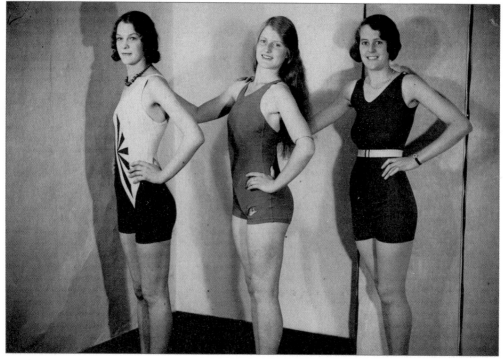

Mind you, swimsuits seem to get skimpier and skimpier. These were fashionable in the late '30s – the front one complete with sunburst motif.

A group of happy holidaymakers photographed in Sutton's old pleasure gardens in July 1952. These gardens were destroyed in the 1953 floods.

By August 1954 the pleasure gardens had been rebuilt and reopened. Here we see the Mayor, Revd Jack Parkinson, opening the Mapleleaf Pool, a gift from the people of Canada.

Hundreds of thousands of children have paddled in the Mapleleaf Pool. These two little girls are Maureen and Janet.

Because the damage caused by the 1953 flood was so extensive, the new sea defences had to be strong!

Hundreds of tons of concrete were poured into these defences which lined the East Coast. Much of the money came from government aid.

In Sutton new beach huts were built on top of the defences. With names like GCHQ, Wyworrie, Atonic and Sunbleste, these beach chalets differ from the old corrugated huts that used to stand in Sutton's Bohemia.

The Sandilands Golf Course had to be relaid.

Originally Sutton's War Memorial was erected on the promenade. In 1955 it was re-erected in the pleasure gardens.

This was the Mablethorpe and Sutton Eisteddfod of 1955, when Mr Houltby (the solicitor) presented the prizes. Also in the picture is a young Revd J.E. Swaby (author of *A History of Louth*).

For the remainder of the '50s Sutton enjoyed that post-war tranquil holiday atmosphere. This photograph was taken by Ken Atterby of Northgate Studios, Louth.

Providing entertainment today is this recently photographed Ladies Theatre Group . . .

. . . just as the Clements did so successfully in Mablethorpe and Skegness.

TRUSTHORPE

It was possible to see the Convalescent Home (Mablethorpe) from Trusthorpe.

The mill at Trusthorpe was one of Lincolnshire's tallest mills comprising eight floors. It was built in 1881 to replace a post mill nearby.

Although it was working well into the twentieth century, modern technology forced it to close.

All that is left is the stump, which has been converted into a private house.

In the 1940s tall radio masts appeared and served as landmarks. Now known as BT Radio Humber, this radio station was so powerful it reached all parts of the globe.

Technology had been greatly accelerated during the Second World War and this enabled radio hams to talk from Hong Kong to South America at a time when telephone communication was restricted.

In 1871 the Convalescent Home between Trusthorpe and Mablethorpe was completed. The idea came from a Miss Emily Anderson, who saw the need to provide holidays for the underprivileged and those recuperating from non-infectious diseases in the Midland counties. The home was opened in June 1871 at a cost of £3,800, and James Fowler of Louth designed the building. Much of the money came from Canon Pretyman, a wealthy clergyman of Great Carlton.

In 1907 a children's wing was added, which enabled a further ten boys and ten girls to stay at the home.

Conditions inside the home were a bit spartan. This was the dining room.

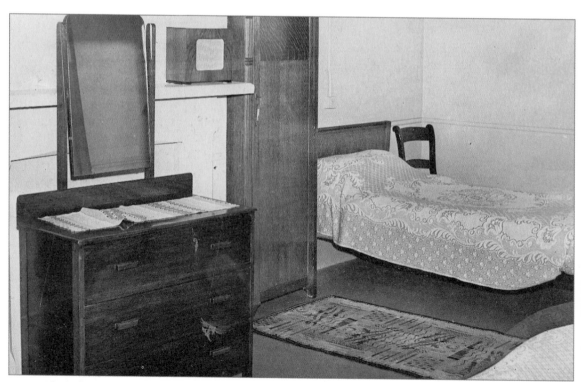

The bedrooms were very basic!

While the sea defences were being built in 1953, rough seas often hampered the work. The Convalescent Home was flooded in 1953, like so many homes along this shore. Rough seas often hampered the work of rebuilding the new defences.

Eventually the defences at Trusthorpe were completed in spring 1954.

The Convalescent Home closed in 1982, was demolished in 1987, and a block of luxury flats known as Queen's Park Close was erected on this site.

In complete contrast, the stumps of a submerged forest can be seen at low tide on this shore, as a reminder that this is an ever changing coastline.

MABLETHORPE

We tend to forget that in Victorian times Mablethorpe was simply a coastal fishing village as this postcard reminds us. It simply says a 'Mablethorpe Fisherman'.

In this aerial shot of Mablethorpe the old
Convalescent Home is visible in the
bottom right-hand corner.

Like Sutton, Mablethorpe came to prominence in Edwardian times as a holiday retreat. This was a view of
the booths and shacks that lined the beach.

Tennyson spent many of his youthful summer holidays in what was then a quiet seaside retreat. His seaside lodging was known locally as Ingoldby House, and was hidden behind some houses off Quebec Road. It was here in 1827 that Charles and Alfred Tennyson retired after their first book, *Poems by Two Brothers*, was published by Jackson's of Louth. Alfred Tennyson was so elated that he roamed the empty sandhills quoting from his own verses.

Pavilion and Sands, Mablethorpe.

The popularity of Mablethorpe as a resort can be seen in this Edwardian postcard, which shows the old lifeboat house on the right of the two helter-skelters, and Clements' entertainment booth in the centre.

Even in Edwardian times there were a few fishing boats left to remind us that Mablethorpe was once a fishing village.

Postcards like this one were sent in their thousands, as the Edwardians loosened the tight corsets of Victorian suppression.

Most of the postcards produced for Mablethorpe reflect this image: donkeys, sun, sea and sand.

This is my favourite Mablethorpe postcard.

Clements the entertainers were a popular feature. They gave two concerts during the day on Mablethorpe beach and one evening performance in the Victoria Road Pavilion.

One of the notable features of the East Coast is the contrast between flat open sands and sky, as demonstrated by this photograph taken from Mablethorpe North End.

The Leicester Children's Holiday Home was started in 1898 by Lady Rolleston, wife of Sir John Rolleston, a well-known Leicester architect. The idea was to give Leicester's underprivileged children a two-week holiday. These holidays became extremely popular and highly sought after. By 1936 this building was erected to cope with the increase in demand. All these years later Englebert Humperdinck (the pop singer) is one of the patrons.

The promenade and pull-over, *c.* 1910.

With the advantage of a railway hundreds of people flocked to this resort. This was the pull-over which was often packed with folk during the summer months.

Bell tents were used for changing, and children enjoyed the freedom of fresh air and close supervision.

A 'kiddies' corner' was introduced on the beach with, just visible in the distance, the old wooden changing huts, which replaced the bell tents. On the top of the concrete steps was a hut known as 'The Old Man's Parliament'.

Once again we see the Louth photographer Les Howe with his two sons, this time sitting in front of the wooden changing huts (now demolished). H.L. Howe (1897–1959) was responsible for taking many of the photographs in this book.

Then there were the donkeys. The pork pie hut in the background has since been removed.

One of the popular attractions was this model railway which operated off High Street from about 1930 up to the Second World War. It was operated by Percy Harding-Kiff.

All along this coast caravans abound. Even in the '50s they were multiplying like rabbits. This was the view of North End. The advent of the caravan was the final nail in the coffin for Mablethorpe's railway, which closed in 1960, and many holidaymakers now towed their own private apartments on the back of their cars to their holiday destinations, much to the annoyance of local guesthouse owners and hotel keepers.

Because of the media coverage during the 1953 floods, Mablethorpe found itself at the centre of attention over the next few years. This was the Trade Fair held in 1954 with the Mayor, Revd Jack Parkinson, looking on.

When the new defences had been installed the Duke of Edinburgh came to inspect them on 14 February 1955. Once again Mayor Jack Parkinson was on hand to meet him. In the background are, left to right, Chief Constable Fowkes, Inspector Charlie Lewis and Sergeant Bray.

After that fateful day in January 1953 everyone had to work quickly before the next high tide in mid-February. Because of the fear of a repetition the Army was rushed to help, and a total of 700,000 tons of slag and rubble were transported from Scunthorpe to plug the gaps in the sea wall.

Even in the face of adversity Mablethorpe residents did not lose their sense of humour. The sign which had been placed in the lounge of a house in the Boulevard simply says 'concealed entrance'! In total an estimated 750,000 tons of sand had been deposited over the flooded area.

The damage that was caused can be seen in this photograph of South Promenade.

This is how it looked before the flood, with the old coastguard look-out hut clearly visible in the background.

Typical of so many homes, 'Sorrento' has its front sitting-room missing. The force of water blew a hole straight through the bungalow.

This was the team responsible for installing the new defences. The photograph was taken at Mablethorpe Sea Bank Park in 1955.

Part of the defence at the Point, Chapel St Leonards, also photographed in 1955.

Hundreds of tons of rubble were deposited all along the coast, and lorries worked day and night to fill the gaps.

People flocked to Mablethorpe, as can be seen by this crowd which came to watch the 1954 Grand Carnival.

Floats were paraded through the town.

Part of the publicity drive to attract more visitors to Mablethorpe in 1955 included this van, which was used as a mobile information unit.

Wilfred Pickles brought his 'Have a Go' radio programme to Mablethorpe in December 1955.

That summer one of the more bizarre spectacles on the beach was an elephant!

These two young girls are enjoying a ride on the old amusements. The dodgem track is in the background.

Roads were widened to make way for increased traffic, such as this road improvement of North End in 1955.

Visitors used to love having their photograph taken on holiday as a souvenir; these were called 'walking photographs'. The two photographers who did much work in the Mablethorpe area were Wrates of Skegness and W. Camm. This is a charming example of Wrates' walking photographs, dated 8 September 1947.

While this is an example of W. Camm's 'Souvenir of a Happy Holiday', taken in the late '50s. The little girl in this snapshot is called Pamela.

A Darby and Joan Christmas party, also photographed by W. Camm & Son of Royal Studios, High Street, 1955.

Old Mr Brownlow spent his lifetime collecting for charity. Here he is pictured outside the Brownlow bungalows with his pram. During the Second World War he collected enough money to pay for two Spitfires!

This was Mablethorpe Primary School in the early '50s.

SECTION SIX

SALTFLEETBY & THEDDLETHORPE

Lieutenant Commander Douglas Valder Duff, the well known boy's adventure storyteller of Theddlethorpe.
He is pictured here to the left of the photograph with a cigarette in his mouth at the Mablethorpe Trade Fair
of 1954. Pictured with him are Tony Stapleton, Mayor Dowdswell and Nellie Spink. Duff's novels created
an end of empire finality mixed with roguish impudence.

The first lifeboat station was established at Theddlethorpe in 1829, moving to Mablethorpe in 1883. Simply manoeuvring the boat into the water was an arduous task. Here we see the *John Rowson Lingard* being lifted into the water with the aid of pulleys, carthorses and plenty of strong lifeboatmen.

When the *John Rowson Lingard* was launched in 1905 by Baroness von Eckarstein, crowds of people flocked to Mablethorpe to watch the ceremony.

Many ships have floundered on this coast. This was the *Emma*, a two-masted barque which came to grief off Mablethorpe in 1902. It was used as a marine museum for a time before being broken up, and its timbers used to prop up the Basin.

In 1907 the *Hera* also came to grief in very nearly the same spot. This time its timbers were used in the walls of the pull-over.

After the *Prussian Queen* floundered off Saltfleetby and was wrecked, its timbers were used in the construction of the present Prussian Queen pub, whose football team is pictured here. Nearby Donna Nook was also named after a ship that was wrecked on this shore.

In 1878 the *Donna Nook* lifeboat was captured on canvas, the painting conveying some of the difficulties lifeboatmen had to experience. In the 1840s a Donna Nook farmer called Richard Hoodless swam his horse through the stormy sea to save four men from a wreck the lifeboat could not reach. He was awarded the silver medal from the Royal Human Society for his bravery.

Even Rimac was named after a brig which was wrecked on this coast in 1874, while on its way from Constadt to Kingston-upon-Hull.

These days Rimac is a nature reserve, and the only place in Lincolnshire where wild orchids can be found. Here we see two workmen repairing steps on the sanctuary. The cost of upkeep is borne by English Heritage and English Nature.

Not all the vessels that floundered on this coast with its shifting sandbanks became wrecks. Here we see a two-masted barque that ran aground off Saltfleetby in the '20s, only to be refloated on the next available high tide.

All along this coast fishermen and anglers can enjoy their sport. There are numerous dykes, ponds and rivers, the banks of which are packed with fishermen during the summer months. This photograph was taken at Vicker's Pond, Saltfleetby, on 28 July 1949.

Most people who lived on this coast enjoyed the 'good life' of self sufficiency and organically grown crops. This was the Bett family of Saltfleetby, who were obviously proud of their chickens.

Saltfleet was a royal port in the Domesday Book. Saltfleet Manor's claim to fame was its connections with Oliver Cromwell at the time of the English Civil War.

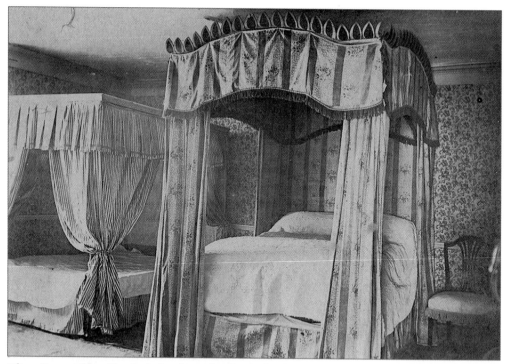

Oliver Cromwell is said to have slept here after the Battle of Winceby.

Downstairs there is a panel behind which Cromwell was supposed to have been concealed.

The annual sale of foals which took place every October has long since ceased. This was Mr Chambers, a grey colt who won the Franklin cup for best foal in the 1935 show.

Despite the disappearance of the foal show, this stretch of coast is still suitable for exercising horses. These horse trials took place at nearby Manby.

Of the three churches in Saltfleetby, Saltfleetby All Saints' is the most unusual. The leaning tower is now leaning even more and the roof over the nave looks as if it is about to break in two. Much of the inside dates from the fifteenth century and it is well worth a visit.

Like so many of these East Coast churches, both Saltfleetby All Saints' and nearby Theddlethorpe All Saints' (shown here) are now redundant. Theddlethorpe was nicknamed the 'cathedral of the marshes'.

All Saints' Mill, Theddlethorpe, *c.* 1911. The mill was later demolished.

But if Theddlethorpe Mill is a reminder of the past, there is hope for the future in Theddlethorpe Primary School. Here we see the children as they prepare for the Big Banana Show on children's television in 1991.

The North Somercotes pancake race is one of the highlights of the village year. Started in 1954 by Lt Col G.S. Grey, it takes place on Shrove Tuesday. Here we see the winner and runner-up on 14 February 1956.

Originally the pancake race was held between residents of North Somercotes and a village in Sussex. Now it is a popular local event, especially with children.

Just as Clarke's ice-creams were well known in the area at the turn of the century, now it is Appleby's. Their headquarters in Conisholme has an ice-cream shop and tea-room. The firm, which also specialises in coach trips and travel, has blossomed in recent years.

At a time when most chapels are left derelict and disused, Conisholme Chapel has had an extension and has been renovated.

The chapel at Marshchapel has been recently restored and now serves as a community centre.

The church in Marshchapel is a particularly fine Perpendicular example of the fifteenth-century church building. The treble bell, re-cast in 1919, bears the names of eight Marshchapel men who died in the First World War. Its bells ring out over some 600 acres of salt 'fitties' reclaimed for Marshchapel and Grainthorpe from the sea.

CLEETHORPES

*'By Jove, how tickled I am to be in Humberside!' On the 8 December 1986 the
Liverpudlian comedian, Ken Dodd remarked. 'In Humberside?' Well, of course this was
before Grimsby and Cleethorpes returned to North Lincolnshire. The last time the Diddy
comic of Notty Ash appeared in Cleethorpes was at Bunny's Nightclub and he always
accredited Humberside as being the first place in Britain where he was considered a
national celebrity. The date was 11 March 1955.*

Cleethorpes enjoyed a good reputation as a seaside resort in Victorian and Edwardian times. This was the slipway to the sea in about 1905.

A favourite pastime with holidaymakers was to hire a boat, which would then have to be dragged into the Humber for an enjoyable trip on the water.

Like Skegness, Cleethorpes had the advantage of a pier which had the pavilion right at the end of it. This photograph was taken from the Cliff Hotel.

On 6 July 1903 disaster struck when the pier caught fire and collapsed. The end-of-pier pavilion was replaced with a new pavilion at the pier entrance.

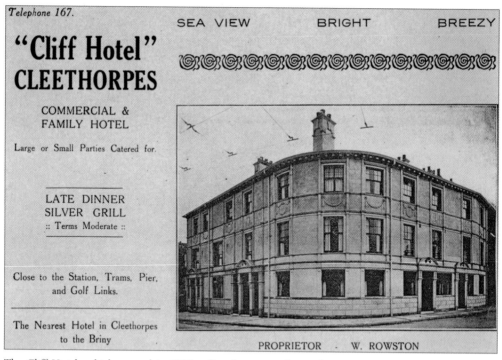

Telephone 167.

SEA VIEW   BRIGHT   BREEZY

"Cliff Hotel" CLEETHORPES

COMMERCIAL & FAMILY HOTEL

Large or Small Parties Catered for.

LATE DINNER
SILVER GRILL
:: Terms Moderate ::

Close to the Station, Trams, Pier, and Golf Links.

The Nearest Hotel in Cleethorpes to the Briny

PROPRIETOR - W. ROWSTON

The Cliff Hotel, which opened in 1863, offered generous hospitality at a price. The building has long ceased to be a hotel and is currently a night club.

Whereas this is a 1960s postcard showing all the development which has took place in the last hundred years.

Because Cleethorpes lay on soft boulder clay, there was constant erosion. In 1902 the houses that faced the sea on Sea Bank road (now Kingsway) lay in danger of falling into the sea. Concrete defences were built to prevent this from happening.

With trams that regularly ran to and from Grimsby, the resort lay within easy reach for most Grimbarians to partake of fresh sea air. Just visible is the cast-iron fountain that marked Queen Victoria's Diamond Jubilee.

Before it was removed to Kingsway the fountain was erected on the sea front. Sadly it was demolished in 1949, and an old landmark disappeared.

Another landmark which has disappeared is the statue of the Boy with the Leaking Boot, originally donated to Cleethorpes by a Swedish Consul, John Carlbom.

The Boy with the Leaking Boot was to Cleethorpes what the Jolly Fisherman was to Skegness. Unfortunately it suffered all forms of vandalism before it was finally removed.

Even on those dreadful postcards of the '50s and '60s he is featured as a symbol of the town.

Throughout the '20s and '30s Cleethorpes built on its reputation as a fun-loving resort. This was the kiddies' sandpit at Thrunscoe recreation ground.

Members of the Howe family have turned up again, this time at the side of the sandpit enjoying a typical day out.

The boating lake . . .

. . . and once again Les Howe, the Louth photographer, and Marion, his wife, are back in the picture.

As hundreds of day-trippers flocked to Cleethorpes, businesses grew and money flooded into the resort.

Trees matured around the boating lake and it was enlarged.

When Cleethorpes became a Borough, Mayor Councillor Sir George Moody JP accepted the Charter in 1936.

It was presented to him by Lord Heneage, who also gave the town its cenotaph in 1919.

One distinctive reminder of the art deco period is the Electricity showroom on Isaac Hill.

By the 1950s deckchairs were in demand on Cleethorpes beach, and parking became something of a problem.

The old Wonderland with its big dipper, dodgems and carousel has been replaced with amusement arcades, *Fantasy World*, bingo parlours and fish and chip shops.

Cleethorpes, like Sutton, Mablethorpe and Skegness, was affected by the 1953 flood. This is a view of the promenade strewn with debris.

On 19 September 1946 A.W. Cox, the Mayor of Cleethorpes, presented the Freedom of the Borough to the Lincolns. Mayor Cox had been Chairman of the Rural district Council of Cleethorpes in 1934/35.

Young army recruits were called in to help clear up the mess in Cleethorpes, just as the group of volunteers below had helped out in Mablethorpe.

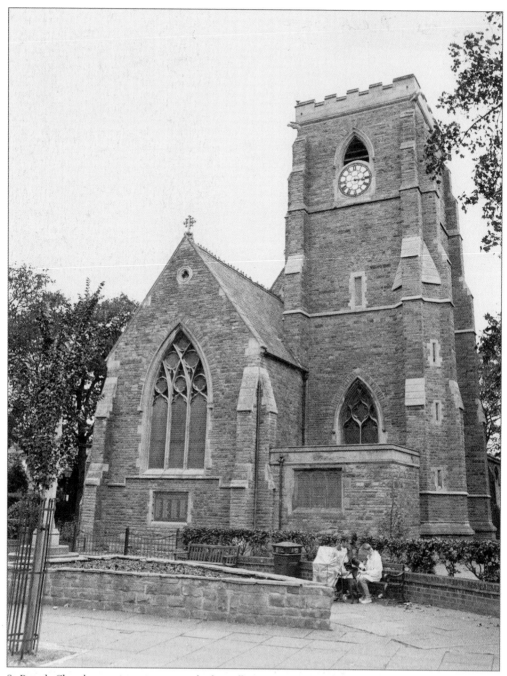

St Peter's Church owes its existence to the boundless energy of the Revd William Price Jones, who was appointed to Clee-cum-Cleethorpes in 1850 at the age of twenty-nine. William Price Jones also organised the building of the vicarage (now part of Church School) and helped to carve some of the stonework in the south wall.

The man in the moon took over as a symbol of the town. Here we see the lights being switched on in 1979 by Mayor Winn.

Cleethorpes has its own model railway, the Cleethorpes Coast Light Railway. This is Chris Shaw, the owner, taking it for a trial run.

Undoubtedly one of the most celebrated events is the Cleethorpes Carnival, held during the last weekend in July. Here we see some revellers outside The Fisherman's Arms in Seaview Street.

In charge of the donkeys is that popular couple Stanley and Gladys Nuttall. This photograph was taken in 1990, when Gladys was Mayor of Cleethorpes.

The Lincolnshire coast is primarily a fun area for children. This photograph was taken at the opening of the new Leisure Centre in Cleethorpes in 1990.

It has indoor sporting facilities and a heated swimming pool. This is the paddling pool for the very young children.

Nearby is the ever popular *Pleasure Island*.

The Point, Chapel St Leonards. When an angry sea lashes against the fine basketwork breakwater it presents a wonderful sight.

ACKNOWLEGEMENTS

There are many people whom I would like to thank for helping me to put this slim volume together, most notably Peter Chambers, Norman Cawkwell, Ben Jacklin, Charles Smith, Geoffrey Roe, Brian Howe and Ken Atterby for allowing me to borrow certain photographs. A special thank you must go to Peter Moore, editor of the *Grimsby Evening Telegraph*, for allowing me to reproduce one or two photos from their archives, and I am extremely indebted to Janet Longden, Peter Chapman and Peter Craig (from the *Grimsby Evening Telegraph*) for their time and patience, not forgetting Louth Secretarial Services who typed this manuscript so carefully.

Part Two
The Lincolnshire Wolds

There was a time when dozens of windmills were dotted about the Wolds, but not any more. In 1852 the miller in Binbrook was Thomas Short. His elder son, William, followed in his father's footsteps and became a miller, while George, the youngest son, became a baker! The windmill was situated at the end of Mount Pleasant (now a Council estate) and slightly proud of the village.

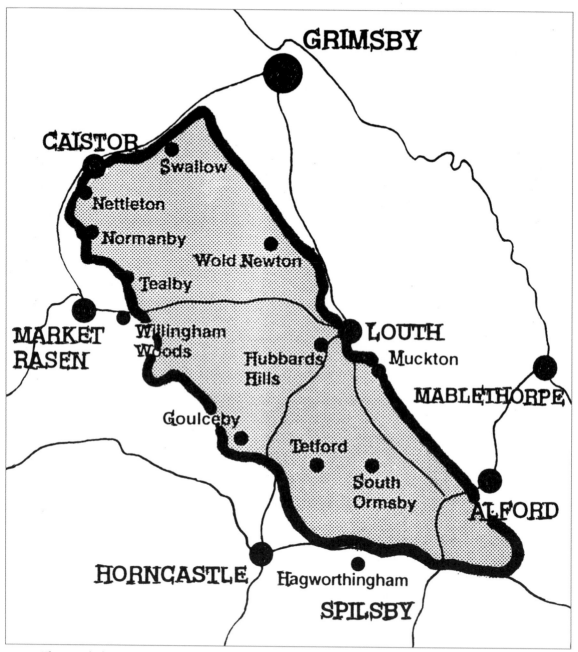

The Lincolnshire Wolds.

INTRODUCTION

Lincolnshire's great secret lies in the Wolds. This rolling undulation, which is more gentle than its near rival and more famous Yorkshire Dales, is mostly unappreciated and yet remains Lincolnshire's great strength.

There are parts of the Wolds where time seems to have stood still for the last hundred years and visitors could find themselves walking in exactly the same landscape as that of the last century. Impressive skies which appear are particularly memorable and range from an ominous black on rainy days to a rainbow selection of sunsets, especially in winter, with every variant in between. It was along these windy roads and deserted fields that T.E. Lawrence found solace when he enrolled at RAF Cranwell; he wanted to hide away from the world and the media of his day. Taking his trusty motorbike (a Brough Superior from Nottingham), he travelled unimpeded through the Wolds to seek inspiration for his book *The Revolt in the Desert* (the abridged version of *The Seven Pillars of Wisdom*), which he completed in Lincoln.*

Lincolnshire is divided up into three administrative parts, known as Kesteven, Holland and Lindsey. The Wolds come into the latter region and rise to a height of 548 ft above sea level. The modern misconception of Lincolnshire as being flat, which still exists today, often confuses anyone who lives on the Wolds.

Curiously enough, there has never been a book written specifically about the Lincolnshire Wolds, although James Hissey's journey through the southern part of Lincolnshire is described in *Over Fen and Wold* (1898). Hissey's meanderings turned into a quest for Tennyson's imaginary Locksley Hall. What he found were bits of Locksley scattered about, such as 'Yonder in that chapel slowly sinking now into the ground' – a reference to Harrington Church, which indeed sinking into the ground in Tennyson's day. The incumbent, the Revd Mr Cracroft, was responsible for saving the church. 'Here is Locksley Hall, my grandson, here the lion guarded gate' is a clear reference to the lion gateway of Scrivelsby. But Tennyson always maintained that both of his poems, 'Locksley Hall' and 'Locksley Hall Sixty Years After', were a compilation of ideas and remembrances rather than any specific place.

In 1851 there were many farmers on the Lincolnshire Wolds who were tenants of 2,000 acres or more – as much land as some squires might own. There was also a marked difference between these farmers and their agricultural labourers, whose average weekly wage was 11s! In the latter part of the century wages improved but even so farm labourers could barely afford home comforts. Often their furniture was of cheap pine (which has recently become fashionable again) and lighting by paraffin lamp.

Although we know the Wolds for its Lincoln Red cattle and Longwool sheep, Lincolnshire was also the home of the early bone-crushing industry. It is sad to think that these early fertilizers should have advanced so much these days that they have become detrimental rather than beneficial. Crushed bones or bone dust were a source of phosphate and nitrogen when applied as a top dressing on light land soils. It worked well too!

Running through the middle of the Wolds is the old Bluestone Heath Road where there are some tranquil views, such as the view from Red Hill (now a nature reserve) near Stenigot or the view from Flint Hill near Scamblesby.

It is not surprising that many famous people have been born on the Wolds – from Sarah Jennings (the first Duke of Marlborough's wife), who was born at Burwell Manor, to Sir Joseph Banks (the botanist), who was born at Revesby. In the twentieth century, Basil Boothroyd, who later became literary editor of *Punch*, worked for some time at a bank in Horncastle before following his literary aspirations, Bernie Taupin (Elton John's lyricist) who went to school at Market Rasen Comprehensive and the actor Jim Broadbent, who won an Oscar for his appearance in *Iris*.

Throughout there has always been the photographer's eagle eye on hand to record events and life in general. It is no wonder this chalk-capped area has been designated an area of outstanding natural beauty, and remains a peaceful haven for anyone wanting to escape the hectic hustle and bustle of everyday life. Long may it continue!

* Lawrence joined the RAF in 1922 under the name of Aircraftsman Ross. After a few months the press got hold of the story and he was dismissed. He then changed his name to Shaw and joined the Tank Corps. After a year he managed to get a transfer to the RAF. He arrived in Cranwell in August 1925 and on occasions spent the night in a lodging house at 33 Steep Hill, Lincoln. The lodging house was kept by a Mrs Dugdale who recalled that one night Lawrence had driven a long distance on his motorcycle in the pouring rain. Mrs Dugdale had a meal ready and said to Lawrence, 'Now just go to the sink and wash your hands and face before you sit down.' 'Good heavens, woman,' said Lawrence, 'God's been washing my face all the way here!' Lawrence left Cranwell for India at the end of 1926.

Before the advent of photography visual images were limited to prints, paintings and engravings. This engraving showed the remains of one of the two ruinous gateways left within the grounds of Belleau Manor. The name of Belleau is derived from the copious spring water which originated here, and Belleau Manor was the home of Sir Henry Vane (1613–62), one-time Governor of Massachusetts (1636–7), MP for Hull and author of *The Retired Man's Meditations*. He was executed in the reign of Charles II.

ALFORD & SPILSBY

This aerial view of Alford shows the Market Place and, to the right, St Wilfrid's Church, which Sir Gilbert
Scott restored in 1867–8. Alford obtained its Market Charter in 1283 when William de Welle was Lord of
the Manor of Alford.

This was West Street in Edwardian times, with some old thatched cottages on the left in front of the Methodist Chapel.

Wesley's brand of Methodism swept through Lincolnshire like a tidal wave, and in this photograph, showing the Lincolnshire Yeomanry in the Market Place, the sign 'Alford Wesleyan Sunday School' is more prominent than anything else.

The view looking back up West Street.

The White Horse Hotel which dates back to the 1600s is on the left-hand side.

Alford is one of the few towns left in Lincolnshire to retain a working windmill. Known as Hoyles' Mill, it was built in 1813 by Sam Oxley and fully restored in 1979 by Mr C. Davis. Here we see a group of Morris men performing at the foot of the mill.

The Windmill Inn in the Market Place (or the Commercial Hotel and Posting House, as it was known) owes its name to a mill, although it is unlikely to have been Hoyles' Mill as the mill depicted here has six sails. Instead it is more likely to be one of the three other Alford windmills, now demolished. It was here at the old Windmill Inn that Thomas Paine established his office as Excise Officer in 1764, a post he held until he was dismissed in 1765. Thomas Paine (1737–1809) wrote two important books, *The Rights of Man* and *The Age of Reason*, and was responsible for preparing the American colonies for independence.

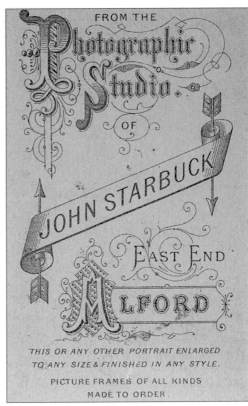

The earliest recorded photographer in Alford was John Starbuck, of East End.

This carte-de-visite portrait of an attractive young woman is an example of his work.

Starbuck's successor, Edwin Nainby, was prolific. This was one of Nainby's studies of the King George V Jubilee celebrations, 1935. It shows Alford Town Band with Russell Barnes as bandmaster and part of the procession in the Market Place. Incidentally, the shop to let in the background was taken over by International Stores.

In the Edwardian golden age, postcards such as this one abounded.

This view of the Market Place looks a bit empty, suggesting, perhaps, that the photograph was taken on a Sunday.

South Market Place, again on a Sunday, perhaps.

Alford has always been noted for its Bull Fair, usually held on the first Thursday in November. This photograph of the auction was taken in 1955.

One of the prize bulls.

Sadly, like so many other cattle markets in Lincolnshire, Alford's cattle market diminished in the '60s and '70s, until it was forced to close in 1987.

Another casualty in Alford has been the War Memorial Hospital, shut in the upheavals of a muddled present-day NHS. The Alford War Memorial Hospital was opened by the Countess of Yarborough in August 1921 in memory of the men from Alford and District who fell in the First World War.

Here we see Remembrance Day in 1955, when Lieutenant D.W. Newsum (Alford Battalion, Royal Lincolnshire Regiment) laid a wreath.

On a lighter note, there were children's parties during the '50s. On this occasion, the pastor is entertaining the children with his Archie Andrews lookalike puppet.

More recently Alford has been revitalized with the craft market. Initially designed by Michael and Heather Ducos for craft exhibitions, it now runs on a regular commercial basis. Here a thatcher demonstrates the almost lost art of thatching.

Bob Oakes, the smithy of Alvingham, demonstrating some ironmongery.

Just a short distance away from Alford is Well Vale. Long the home of the Rawnsley family (the last Mrs Rawnsley died in 1978), in more recent times it was owned by Mr Reeve who preferred to live in a smaller modern house within the grounds rather than at the hall. The hall is currently owned by Maypole School which was founded in 1884 in Horncastle.

The grounds and lake are peaceful, as can be seen in this photograph.

Not far from Alford and nestling neatly on the edge of the Wolds is the small market town of Spilsby, with a statue of John Franklin dominating the western side of the Market Place.

Sir John Franklin (1786–1847), the Spilsby-born Arctic explorer, spent two years at Louth Grammar School before joining the Navy at the age of fourteen. He saw action at the Battle of Copenhagen in 1801, and two months later was appointed midshipman under another Lincolnshire man, Captain Matthew Flinders. During an illustrious career in the Navy, his ultimate achievement was to be credited with discovering the North-West Passage. His body was never found.

At the turn of the twentieth century A. Greetham was the saddler, but his business days were numbered as the age of motor traffic loomed on the horizon.

Aware of the possibilities of this new form of transport was J.A. Badley. His business as cycle agent and motor car dealer was operated from The Terrace, which was near Main Road, Spilsby.

On the east side of the Market Place is Spilsby's famous Market Cross, dating back originally to the fourteenth century.

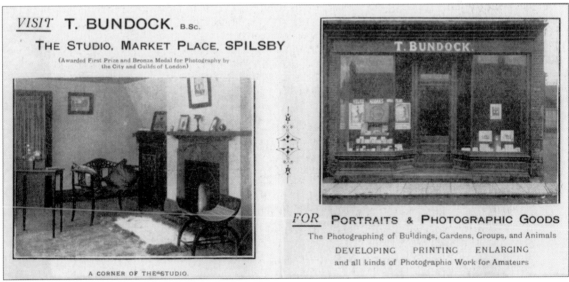

Although Edwin Nainby had a photograpic studio in Spilsby, the main photographer in the town was T. Bundock of the Market Place.

During the First World War the 5th Lincolns had an OC training camp at Spilsby. Here we see Colonel Beaumont Walker enjoying some refreshment between sorties.

Captain Bell and Major Marshall (with his Field Marshal Haig stance).

A group of young officers of 'B' Company.

There was little time to take photographs in those hectic days of the First World War except in moments of relaxation. I wonder if these two had any idea of what they would walk into when they went on active service?

Of the many fine houses that surrounded Spilsby only a handful are left, including Dalby Hall. The original Hall was destroyed by fire in the eighteenth century and the new Hall was built in 1856 to the designs of James Fowler, of Louth.

Dalby Hall should not be confused with Dalby Grange, the home of Peter Middleton, which is a farmhouse in the old-fashioned sense of the word.

Another fine house in the Spilsby area is Revesby Abbey, which escaped demolition only by a whisker. This house was built on the site of Sir Joseph Banks' house, which in turn was built on the site of the Abbot's House of Revesby Abbey. Remains of the old Cistercian abbey have long since disappeared.

This is the author standing in the porch just outside the front entrance in 1974 to give the reader some idea of size. This enormous pile was built in the 1840s by J. Banks-Stanhope and since the early 1960s has been left unoccupied and derelict.

The old East Lincolnshire Railway line carefully skirted the Wolds. On the east side from Boston to Grimsby it went through Sibsey, Old Leake, East Ville, Little Steeping and Firsby, looping around Willoughby, Alford, Aby, Authorpe, Legbourne and Louth before straightening up for Grimsby. This was Firsby Junction, where it was possible to change for Spilsby, in 1954.

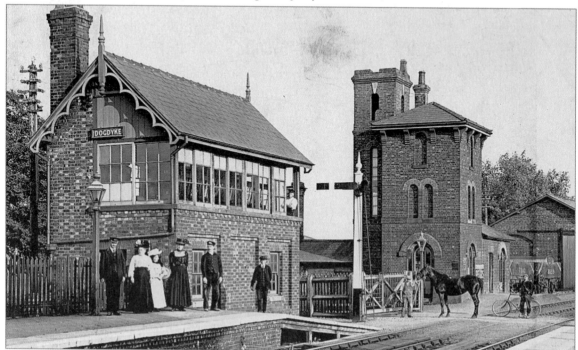

The other line from Boston to Lincoln went through Langrick, Dogdyke, Tattershall, Woodhall, Kirkstead (change for Horncastle), Stixwould, Southrey and Bardney on its way to Lincoln. This was Dogdyke station at the turn of the twentieth century.

THE TENNYSON LEGACY

Alfred Tennyson was born on 6 August 1809 at Somersby Rectory, the fourth of twelve children of the then rector, George Clayton Tennyson, and his wife, Elizabeth, a daughter of Stephen Fytche, vicar of Louth.

George Clayton Tennyson (sometimes referred to as the Doctor) was rector of Somersby and Bag Enderby churches. During Tennyson's time at Somersby, the roof of the church was thatched, but was subsequently tiled in one of the two nineteenth-century restorations.

It was here that the young Alfred Lord Tennyson was baptised and, as a boy, helped to toll the bell.

In the graveyard, Tennyson was reputed to have scratched the words 'Byron is dead' on a rock in 1824, close by the fifteenth-century cross.

Dr Tennyson's other church of Bag Enderby was more spartan than Somersby, but he livened it up with remarkable sermons. One local was heard to remark: 'E read 'em from a paaper and I didn't know what 'e meant.' George Clayton Tennyson had taken his degree as a Doctor of Civil Law in 1813.

Reminders of Alfred Tennyson's time in Somersby abound, such as 'The Brook', depicted romantically on this postcard.

This photograph of the babbling brook is vastly different from the brook that is left today. (Incidentally, Tennyson's famous poem 'The Brook' had to be rescued from the wastepaper bin!)

Stockwith Mill (on the road to Hagworthingham) still survives as a tea-room and gift shop. Local gossip has it that the mill inspired Tennyson's poem 'The Miller's Daughter' but I can find no evidence of this. Indeed, references in 'The Miller's Daughter' point to Hubbard's Hills' windmill (now demolished). There was a watermill less than a hundred yards away, which ground flour on days when there wasn't enough wind. 'Where this old mansion mounted high looks down upon the village spire' was more likely to be Thorpe Hall and 'The white chalk-quarry from the Hill' could either have been Hubbard's Hills or the quarry just off London Road.

Other pieces of Tennyson memorabilia, such as this thatched cottage in Bag Enderby, have gone.

The woodcutter's cottage still survives, echoing a timeless reminder that much of the countryside around this area has changed little in the last 150 years.

Next to Somersby Rectory is the Vanbrugh creation of Somersby Grange. This family group was photographed by Edwin Nainby of Alford in about 1900.

Another village with Tennyson connections is Tealby. It is here that the River Rase comes fresh from its source at Bully Hill.

It was also here that Charles Tennyson d'Eyncourt (Alfred Tennyson's uncle) built Bayons Manor on the site of the old manor in 1830. Imposing and solid as it was, with castellated battlements, Bayons Manor was eventually blown up with dynamite in the mid-1960s.

The grandiose setting of Charles Tennyson d'Eyncourt's Bayons Manor is further demonstrated in this photograph of moat, drawbridge and portcullis! In 1807 a labourer discovered an earthenware pot containing 6,000 Henry II silver pennies while ploughing a field on the Tennyson estate. Some of the coins ended up in the British Museum.

Charles Tennyson (Alfred's elder brother) was vicar of Grasby for about forty years. Grasby lies on the western edge of the Wolds with some fine views of Caistor and beyond. Charles Tennyson arrived in Grasby in 1835 as Charles Tennyson Turner, after succeeding to the estate of his great-uncle, Samuel Turner of Caistor. In 1837 he was joined in Grasby by his young wife Louisa, a niece of Sir John Franklin and sister of Emily Sellwood, later to become Alfred Tennyson's wife.

A rare photograph of Lady Tennyson d'Eyncourt addressing a group of girl scouts in Louth in the late '20s. She accepted the invitation from Mrs Oscar Dixon of Abbey House, Louth.

This would have been Alfred Tennyson's first view of Louth as he travelled along the London Road to attend Louth Grammar School. The gradient of the road would have been a little steeper in his day. It was Napoleonic prisoners of war who hacked out the chalk to lower the road (in about 1810 to 1815), so making the journey less perilous for stagecoaches and horse-drawn carts.

Although the group of Louth Grammar School boys in School House Lane was photographed in 1860, it would not have differed greatly from any group in Tennyson's day.

LOUTH &
LITTLE CAWTHORPE

Louth has sometimes been referred to as the capital of the Wolds. Much of its wealth originally came from wool, and farmers have used it as a trade centre for the last 500 years. Here we see the cattle market in about 1905.

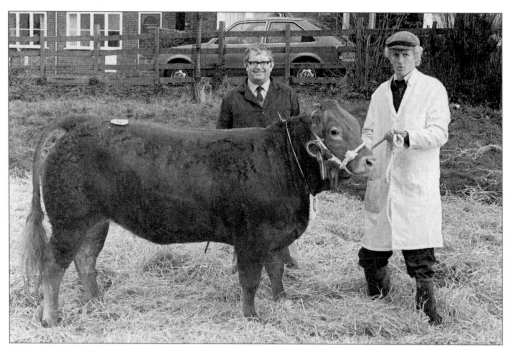

Although the cattle market is no longer the bustling, busy centre that it was, there are still auctions and a Christmas stock show. Dennis and Stephen Nundy of Lincross are showing off their champion 'beast' in this photograph.

The Union Workhouse, or 'Poorhouse', as it was known locally, was built in 1837 to house 300 paupers. It is now Louth County Hospital, but many people of the older generation were reluctant to use it because of its past connotations. A Louth woman, Mrs Janetta Norwebb, who died in Brigg Poorhouse in 1817, numbered among her most intimate acquaintances Laurence Sterne, the author of *Tristram Shandy*.

The Louth Volunteers were formed in 1814. This photograph of a group of sergeants by Plumtree was taken in about 1870.

Even at the turn of the twentieth century, after the Boer War, the Volunteers were still going strong. They often met at the Cow Pastures or the rifle range (commonly known as 'The Butts') off the South Elkington road. The Volunteers eventually amalgamated with Louth Rifle Club.

Carved out of the Wolds by the River Lud is a natural beauty spot known as Hubbard's Hills (it was called Hubbard's Valley in Victorian times). Even when this photograph was taken, in about 1890, it served as a peaceful haven.

Just a short distance from Hubbard's Hills is the tollbar on the Horncastle Road. The 1770 Tolls Act allowed for charges to be made for horse-drawn traffic. There were certain exceptions, such as the Royal Mail, clergy visiting the sick, or people attending a church service or worship.

In the early part of this century the tollbar house was the home of Bill Cribb (1902–47). He was the son of Mr Cribb the solicitor, whose office was above Strawson's shop in the Market Place.

Of all the photographers working in Louth probably the most prolific was Arthur James of Ramsgate House. This delightful 'Lincolnshire worthy' was photographed in about 1880.

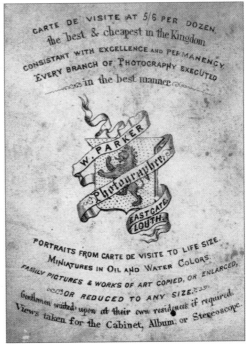

This Victorian couple have obviously donned their best clothes for the photograph.

The back of W. Parker's carte-de-visite.

This was the reverse of Arthur James' carte-de-visite, showing his premises in Ramsgate, which were sadly demolished by the flood in 1920.

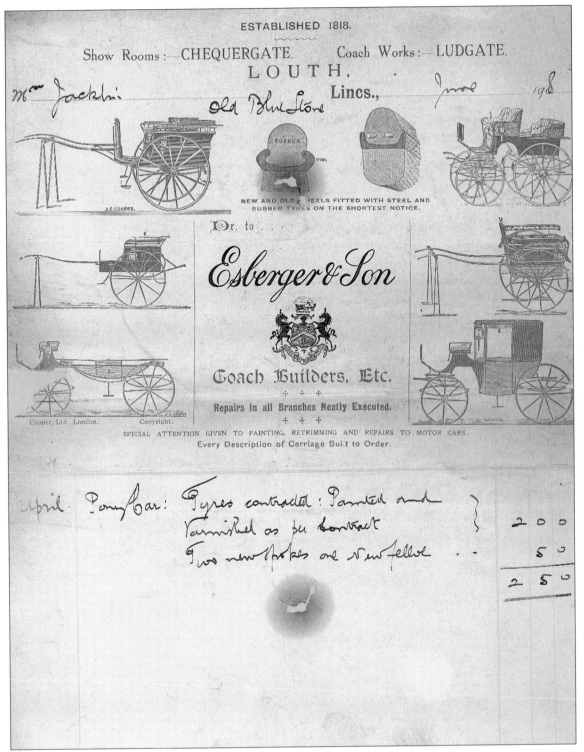

In the nineteenth century Louth had three firms of coachbuilders, Thorn's, Richardson's and Esberger's. This was Esberger's bill depicting their comprehensive selection of carriages.

Although overshadowed by the more famous boys' school, King Edward VI Girls' Grammar School has also produced a selection of notable old girls, sometimes forgotten in the wake of their husbands' illustrious careers. Here we see the tennis team of 1911 comprising from left to right, G. Wright, L. Southern, R. Smith and E. Bach.

Nor did the girls just stick to tennis: this was the cricket team of 1911! Back row, left to right: S. Yates, M. Oldroyd, Nora Lane, Rose Robinson, Mabel ?, -?-. Front row: Miss Millson, A. Wright, Miss M. Millson, Miss Marshall and P. Taylor.

Here we see the Bank Holiday meet of the Southwold Hunt in the Cornmarket, Louth, in 1954.

It is the Boxing Day meet of the Southwold Hunt at the cattle market that sticks in my mind. This was one of the highlights of the year and a fixed date in many people's calendars, reliving the century-old tradition.

Just a short distance away from Louth is Little Cawthorpe, with its manor house and pub, the Royal Oak (nicknamed The Splash by many locals). The village was awarded the title of Best Kept Small Village in Lincolnshire in 1988.

Between Little Cawthorpe and Legbourne is Watery Lane, which was a short-cut in Edwardian times. Here we see Cornelius Potts (taxi driver from the Mason's Arms) navigating the shallow stream in his pony and trap.

This is the source of the Great Eau, and it was possibly for dogcarts and even motor cars to drive down it. This photograph dates from about 1926.

Life was hard in Edwardian times and many local residents of Little Cawthorpe had to look to the land for sustenance. Here we see old Mrs Barton, who kept chickens at one end of Watery Lane.

Mr James Barton, the postman, outside his house in Cawthorpe.

Here we see a Conservative Party raffle in front of the Jacobean manor house. The photo was taken in the '50s with the Revd Mr Swaby (who wrote *A History of Louth*) on the extreme left. In the centre of the photograph is the late Cyril Osborne, MP for Louth, buying a raffle ticket and Mr Sophus Nielsen (in spectacles) immediately behind him.

Cawthorpe Manor bears the crest of the ill-fated Mottram family, who were wiped out by smallpox. Inside the house (this is the drawing room) is a rich array of carved woodwork, some of which may have come from nearby Legbourne Abbey after the Dissolution of the Monasteries. For more than a century it was the family home of the Mortons who, among other things, trained one of Edward VIII's racehorses during the early part of this century. Then it became the family home of the Nielsons before the current owners, Mr and Mrs Charles Grant and family, moved in.

The pond, just in front of the Manor House, made a tranquil picture.

LIFE ON THE WOLDS

Life on the Wolds at the turn of the century was hard in many respects, yet it had its rewards. Most families 'made do' with their slim resources, and couples who had their photographs taken liked to be seen in their Sunday best.

There was little crime and if the police had to be contacted the matter was obviously serious. This smart police station sergeant was photographed in about 1870.

The Round house (Langton-by-Partney) is one of the few conical thatched cottages left in Lincolnshire. This picturesque example is one of only a handful still standing in the county.

There were few vehicles on Lincolnshire's roads in the fifties. Here we see a wonderful example of an old Lanchester parked up on the side of the road belonging to Mr and Mrs Krogh Nielsen.

One of the most important battles of the English Civil War took place at Winceby in 1643. This was a view of the battlefield taken in the 1960s.

Carts or wagons were used to transport hay or crops.

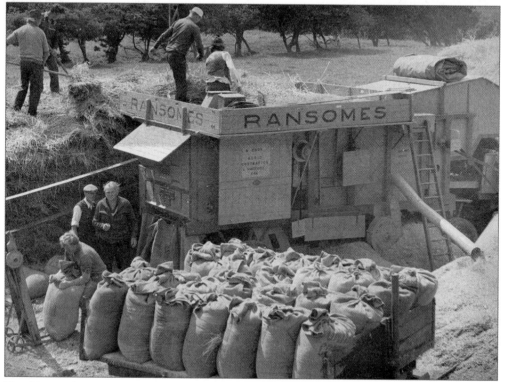

Threshing machines were put into operation at harvest.

This delightful photograph of Tom Barton, the Ludford butcher, with his son Arthur, was taken in about 1903. The Bartons lived at Ivy House, Ludford.

During the First World War there were country shoots. This photograph, of about 1916, was taken in the Binbrook/Rothwell area.

Alternatively there was rabbiting. This was C. ('Gyp') Parker photographed in 1914 with his sack on his back.

Up to the First World War, most people viewed the Wolds via pony and trap. The horse in this photograph is Mustang.

The advances in automobility saw a new mode of transport, the motorcycle, sometimes with side-car, such as this brand new Indian in 1915.

Corn stooks lined the fields in the inter-war years on the Wolds.

At this Conservative dinner in the late '30s we can see the familiar figure of Major J. St Vigor-Fox (in grey suit), fourth from right. He was High Steward of Louth and lived at Girsby Manor. Next to him (the smaller gentleman, third from the right) is Lieutenant Colonel A.P. Heneage MP, who came from Hainton Hall but lived for most of his life at nearby Walesby Hall.

Girsby Manor was demolished after a Mr Holmes of Wragby bought the house and stripped it of its wood and lead. Subsequently it became unsafe and had to be knocked down.

Hainton Hall, where the Heneage family had lived for generations, did not fare too well either, although at least most of it is still standing. A large chunk of it was altered when dry rot was discovered in the '50s.

Before the days of the drink-drive laws came into force many Wold pubs became popular drinking haunts. One example was The Blue Bell, Belchford (recently renovated) which was noticeable by its replica of a huge bell displayed outside.

There are many memorable public houses dotted throughout the Wolds. The White Hart, Tetford, dates from about 1520 and it was here that the famous Dr Johnson reputedly drank. Other village pubs that spring to mind are the Three Horseshoes, Goulceby, the Durham Ox, Thimbleby, the Sebastopol, Minting, the Nickerson Arms, Rothwell, the King's Head, Tealby, and the Vine, South Thoresby.

Farming methods were to change in the post-Second World War era. Here we see Bill Massey, Ralph Baumber and George Hallgath in front of their first combine harvester at Driby in 1955.

Many people still hankered after the old way of life. This splendid photograph of Harold Baldock with his twenty-one-year-old mare, Judy, was taken as late as 1996. He is seen ploughing his farm at North Willingham.

The post-war advance in farming meant that there was much crop-spraying to increase yield. This is a field of barley. It is only recently that we have come to understand that perhaps the old way of farming was best, as more and more people turn to organic foods.

Had farmers or the financial institutions that own farms stuck to more conventional methods the nation would be a lot healthier. There was nothing wrong with those old labour-intensive methods: harvesting in 1956 is seen here.

Artificial fertilizers have done much damage to the land and even more damage to the NHS, as puzzled doctors find new ailments caused either directly or indirectly by these chemicals. Clues only came to light after crop-spraying aeroplanes went off course and sprayed people rather than crops.

Whether harvesting was worth taking to this extreme is questionable. Gluts in production, owing to over-generous subsidies, often meant that Britain landed up with grain mountains. This meant that Britain fed Russia or Poland or some obscure country just to use up the excess before it went mouldy. But at least the price was kept high!

Atrocities committed in the post-war era in the name of progress could only be put down to greed. The sign on this snow-covered field is self-explanatory.

If chemicals hit the vegetable crop, with any overspill of effluent entering the water supply, there was even worse to come with BSE (or mad cow disease). Here we see a Lincoln Red heifer and her calf.

In this photograph the Lincoln Red Cattle Society are safely perched on a hayrick well out of reach of the cattle.

To keep cattle in, a series of cattle grids were built in the '50s and '60s. Here we see a typical cattle grid being built at Driby with, from left to right, Phil Olivant, John Mountain, Jim Roper and George Hallgath.

Occasionally there were farming demonstrations to show the machines that replaced horsepower in the 1970s. Did they reassure farmers that they were adopting the right attitudes? The International Junior pictured here was a throwback to a bygone age.

I'm not sure the farmers shown here were entirely convinced as they studied a tractor going through its paces.

One great character was the late Eric Ranby of Grimblethorpe Hall, born at Bilsby Hall near Alford. He was a fiercely independent farmer whose actions sometimes bordered on the eccentric.

Electricity did not reach some Wold villages until after the Second World War. Here we see an electricity van in Thoresway off to repair a broken cable. Before the advent of the electric light, candles were used for lighting and open fires for heat. On the left is the old wheelhouse with its water wheel which has long since been dormant. An amazing AA sign on the side of the wheelhouse states that Thoresby is 155¼ miles from London! Farmers frequently had to harness a stream or running water to create energy to run their threshing machines. The barn in this case was on the other side of the road, and a shaft was built beneath the road to drive the threshing machine. It was built in 1813 and last used in the 1930s.

Because the Wolds are so undulating many dips and hollows are prone to flooding. Here we see a lorry negotiating the road out of North Willingham, which is awash with rainwater.

Lincolnshire is well known for its huntin', shootin' and fishin' set. Here we see two local squires: Will Haggas of the Walmsgate estate (left) and David Haxby of Ketsby.

Another possible sport or pastime which may become a thing of the past is fox-hunting. Here we see the South Wold Hunt going through Welton-le-Wold on their Boxing Day Meet.

Two adamant and aggressive Anti-Hunt League protestors questioning the morality of fox-hunting.

Another sight that we shall see no more – stubble burning; it was banned in 1994!

One or two villages have adopted the word 'wold' into their names, such as Welton-le-Wold. This is Welton Vale (the road leading to Welton-le-Wold), *c.* 1900.

Other villages such as Wold Newton or Barnetby-le-Wold (seen here) have acquired a wold attachment to separate them from other villages of the same name.

There are many villages and towns with the suffix 'thorpe' or 'by' from Lincolnshire's time under Danelaw. In the northern part of the Wolds the name of Thor appears as a prefix quite regularly, as in North Thoresby, Thorganby, Thoresway and Thornton-le-Moor. In Norse mythology Thor was the God of Peasants and the lower classes (he was also their God of Thunder!). This delightful photograph of Thoresway was taken in the '50s.

Basically the Lincolnshire Wolds comprise farmers and their produce. This is the weekly auction held in the Cornmarket, Louth, under the watchful gaze of auctioneer Charles Thompson.

These four spring onions, grown by Walter Phillips of Barnetby, are fine examples of home-grown produce. The judge Geoffrey Houltby (right) is accompanied by steward Archie Eastcrabbe and his assistant Brian Wood.

Here we see Mrs A. Heneage (wife of the Louth MP Lieut.Col. Sir Arthur Heneage) at the Conservative Horse Show of 1933. It was held at North Thoresby and Mrs Heneage was asked to present the prizes.

HORNCASTLE & CADWELL

Horncastle once had the biggest horse-fair in the country, and George Borrow refers to a horsey connection in the town in his book, The Romany Rye *of 1857.*

The Bull Ring had a healthy cluster of hostelries surrounding it.

St Mary's Church is neatly hidden away. This view of it from St Mary's Square was taken by W.K. Morton. During the Civil War Cavalier Sir Ingram Hopton was buried in this church on Cromwell's instructions, after he had been killed at the Battle of Winceby.

There was a marked contrast between the workers' cottages and the larger more ornate country houses such as Baumber Park. Before the First World War this was owned by the Sharpe family.

At the turn of the twentieth century Horncastle comprised many small cottages often with pantiled roofs, as can be seen in this selection off Spilsby Road.

One of the most memorable roads into Horncastle from Louth is through the Wolds. Cawkwell Hill is a landmark. I defy anyone who thinks that the whole of Lincolnshire is flat to climb Cawkwell Hill and think again!

A couple of miles outside Horncastle lies Scrivelsby, the ancestral home of the Kings' Champion, whose role is to defend the monarch's right to the throne against challenges. This feudal tradition, once held by the Marmions, is continued to this day by the Dymoke family. This is the Lion gateway, in about 1925.

The name of Marmion is still retained in the Marmion Arms at Haltham.

The original Scrivelsby Court, ancient home of the Dymokes, caught fire in the reign of George III and most of the old manor, including the great hall, was destroyed. This photograph shows the later Manor, which fell into disrepair and was demolished in the 1950s, leaving the present Dymokes to live in a conversion of one of the gatehouses of the original Scivelsby Court.

Just a short distance away from Scrivelsby (between Dalderby and Scrivelsby) lay this unique cottage known as Tea Pot Hall. It burned down in 1945. The photograph was taken by Hugh Martineau, who took many of the photographs in this book.

The late Hugh Martineau was a schoolmaster by profession. He taught at St Hugh's School, Woodhall Spa for over twenty years, where his nickname was far from complimentary. Latterly he can be remembered for his many contributions to *Lincolnshire Life* both as a writer and as a photographer.

The most recent event to capture the public's attention was the World Ploughing Championships, which were held just outside Horncastle in 1984.

A view of the ploughing parade marching through the town, September 1984.

Everyone who attended the event needed feeding, but it was unrecorded whether these three were eating a ploughman's!

Formerly known as Cadwell Vale, it was here that Cadwell Hall once stood – until it was demolished in 1921. The grounds of the estate became a motorcycle track in 1934, the brainchild of the Wilkinson family.

Cadwell Hall was the country seat of the Allenby family, of which General Edmund Henry Hynman Allenby (1861–1936) was a member. He had two uncles who were landowners in the area, Everitt Allenby of Fotherby and Hynman Allenby of Kenwick Hall, and an aunt who lived in George Street, Louth.

Cadwell Vale soon became a popular venue with local motorcycle enthusiasts and, more recently, world champions such as Mike Hailwood, Barry Sheene, Giacomo Agostini, Wayne Gardner and Roger Marshall have ridden on this circuit.

Cadwell Park is well known throughout Europe for its motorcycle races. This photograph, of about 1955, shows just how popular this sport had become.

Cadwell Park is not just confined to motorcycles, as can be seen in this photograph of two vintage cars going around the track.

SOME WOLD CHURCHES

*St Olave's, Ruckland, was practically rebuilt in 1885 from designs by architect W. Scorer at a cost of £400.
There is a distinctive rose window in the west wall.*

The Revd George Hall (1863–1918) was vicar at St Olave's, Ruckland, from 1905 to 1918. He wrote *The Gypsy Parson*, published in 1915 by Sampson Low Marston & Co.

All Saints' Church, Haugham, was modelled on St James' Church, Louth, and its spire can be very confusing, especially when driving to Louth on the A16 from Boston: it is such a good replica that many a traveller has muddled the two spires. This photograph was taken in about 1870.

Although largely redundant the church is still occasionally used, as can be seen at this baptism of 1993.

St Vedast's, Tathwell, was named after the sixth-century French bishop, and much of the Norman building was retained in the 1889 restoration. The obelisk to the right of the photograph is a monument to Lord William Henry Cavendish Bentinck (1804–70), one of the sons of the fourth Duke of Portland.

The Hamby memorial inside is an imposing monument of alabaster erected in 1627, depicting William Hamby kneeling at a desk and Edward and Elizabeth Hamby at another desk below. Jean Howard, curator of Louth Museum and a champion of old memorials, is standing in the foreground of the photograph.

At Raithby-with-Hallington, snugly tucked into the foothills of the Wolds, is the delightful church of St Peter. It was completely rebuilt in 1839 by the Revd Henry Chaplin at his own expense, although the beautiful fourteenth-century font was retained. The Revd Mr Nunnally was rector of Raithby from 1959 to 1978.

This delightful setting of St Mary's Church, Harrington, shows the tower peeping over the trees. It is reached by the road, not by the Hall! Harrington Hall was rebuilt by the Amcotts family in 1673 on the medieval foundations of the old Coppledick family seat. It was also here that Tennyson was inspired to write 'Come into the garden, Maud', dedicated to Rosa Baring (a member of the eminent banking family), who lived at Harrington for a number of years.

St John the Baptist Church, Belleau, was another church almost completely rebuilt in 1862 while retaining its medieval font. The original church on this site was built by Ralph West of Claythorpe between 1307 and 1327.

Some Wold churches have fared better than others. When I last visited All Saints', Oxcombe, the church was in a poor state of repair with notices warning of falling masonry.

Holy Trinity, Muckton, may have been demolished, but these two delightful photographs remain of Mrs Surgey, wife of the vicar. Herbert Henry Surgey was the incumbent from 1905 to 1914.

This delightful photograph taken of Mrs Surgey was taken in the rectory grounds.

St Michael's Church, Driby, could easily have gone the same way, but has since been converted into a Gothic revival private residence by London barrister Keith Walmsley.

There are many fine examples of fonts in Lincolnshire churches. The octagonal font in Bag Enderby church with its representations of the Pieta – Christ's mother holding on her knees the body of her son taken from the cross – a seated figure with a lute and a fox, part of Lincolnshire folklore.

All Saints' Church, Hameringham, 3½ miles from Horncastle. The name Hameringham means village on the hill and the church contains a Jacobean pulpit with the original hourglass in its stand – presumably to remind the vicar not to preach too long!

The village of Burwell was once a busy market town. This photograph of it was taken in the '50s, showing the butter cross in the far distance. The church of St Michael is a short distance away from the village.

About the only reminder of Burwell's importance is the old red-brick butter cross, which served as a dovecote for a number of years and is now used as a church hall.

Here we see Mrs Surgey (once again) and Mrs Watson standing outside the entrance to Burwell Church.

This more modern photograph shows the Revd Peter Fluck (half-brother of the late Diana Dors) inspecting an old door. Peter Fluck was rector of the South Ormsby group of churches from 1975 to 1984.

Mr Fluck was a resourceful and down-to-earth cleric who will long be remembered in this area for holding services in the Massingberd Arms pub! Many so-called Christian vicars may take note; it's not the church or material surroundings that matter but Christian principles, thought and conscience that should be paramount in a service of worship.

The delightful church of St Andrew in Donington on Bain has changed little since this photograph was taken in about 1910.

The church at Thoresway near Binbrook, which had an idyllic setting, has had the indignity of a modern house built just to the right of this photograph, in front of the church.

At least it has fared better than Calceby church. All that is left of the Church of St Andrew, which is mentioned in the Domesday Book, are these few stones. The last service was held in this church in about 1692.

Inside St Helen's Church, North Thoresby, is a memorial to Francis Bond (1850–1918), an authority on church architecture, fonts and woodcarving, who was born in North Thoresby.

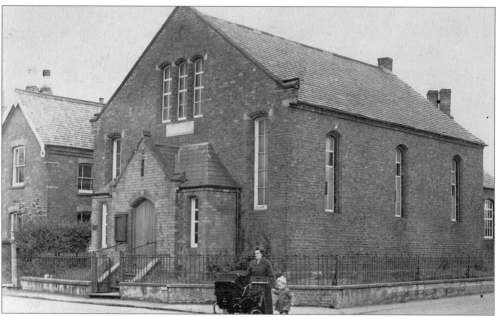

As well as churches, there are many fine examples of chapels still standing. This is the 1846 Methodist Chapel at North Thoresby, but other examples can be found throughout the county.

Probably the most impressive parish church in the Wolds is St James', Louth, seen here in 1934. It has the tallest parish church spire in England and is one of the few parishes to have had its vicar hanged, drawn and quartered. Thomas Kendall suffered this fate for his part in the Lincolnshire Rising of 1536.

Here we see Owen Price, long-time organist of St James' (1897–1946), choirmaster and music teacher. The photograph was taken on 4 April 1940.

The smallest church in Lincolnshire is Linwood Methodist Church, a wooden construction covered by sheet-metal strips. In 1962 the Rev Siddle was minister in charge.

All Saints', Walesby, has often been nicknamed 'the ramblers' church' because of its situation. Among the list of former rectors is the name of the Revd R. Burton, author of *The Anatomy of Melancholy* – just the sort of book to cheer up any worn-out rambler!

Another Wold church with RAF connections is Ludford. It is yet another James Fowler-designed church, and like Binbrook St Mary and St Peter is a combination of two previous churches, which once served Ludford Parva and Ludford Magna.

To commemorate the crew of Lancaster PB476, No. 12 Squadron, RAF Wickenby, a small stone memorial was unveiled by Trevor Budworth (of the Lincolnshire Military Preservation Society) and Padre Ivor Haythorne. There are many such memorials honouring the RAF dotted about the Wolds, often by the roadside.

The delightful church of St Mary and St Gabriel in Binbrook stands as a tribute to that prolific Victorian architect James Fowler. Two previous churches combined to make one, and it was consecrated in 1869. Inside there is a stained glass window commemorating its close ties with RAF Binbrook.

MARKET RASEN,
BINBROOK & CAISTOR

Looking down King Street, Market Rasen, at the turn of the last century. The Greyhound Inn (one of the oldest pubs in the area, established in 1639) on the left of the photo advertises 'stabling or billiards together with Ind Coope's ales and stouts delivered in cask and bottle'.

The Greyhound, in the late '50s or early '60s. The photograph shows that the pub had become a café! It is now known as The Chase.

Market Rasen has a good golf course and excellent tennis club. Here we see some early members of the tennis club in about 1911.

Market Rasen is well known for three things: its railway station, its racecourse and de Aston School. Here the railway station is having a new roof erected in 1941. Unfortunately the roof was built in a hurry during those hectic war years.

Fiery Sun was the winner of the Wainfleet Selling Handicap Hurdle held at Market Rasen racecourse on 23 September 1989. From left to right are Paul Matthews, John Maltby, *Fiery Sun* (trained by G. Oldroyd), the head lad, John Martin, and Gordon Kirk.

The Market Place, with its pump and cobbles, shows us how Market Rasen differs from Middle Rasen and West Rasen.

Probably the most impressive chapel still standing in the Wolds is the Centenary Methodist Chapel in Market Rasen. It stands at one end of Union Street, and its neo-classical theme is rather reminiscent of Willingham Hall.

Willingham Hall was the home of the Boucherett family for over a hundred years. Latterly it was used as a training centre by Lindsey Civil Defence Corps before being blown up (like Bayons Manor) in the early '60s.

Arthur Mee described Binbrook in his *King's England – Lincolnshire*: 'The broach spire of the church rising above the trees and the red-pantiled roofs of the houses make an attractive rural picture; and pleasing, too, the little market square, redolent of other days.'

Set in the centre of Binbrook is the Georgian Manor House which was long the family home of the Johnsons and latterly the Clarkes. This back view of the Manor was taken in 1904.

Woodthorpe Johnson Clarke (1856–1916) in between two 'Edwardian Roses' on the tennis court of Binbrook Manor, 1907.

The Clarkes were friendly with the Player family from Nottingham. Here we see Violet Clarke and Mrs Player in 1909.

This unusual photograph shows Edwardian ladies retiring from the garden at Binbrook Manor. Mrs Player is on the extreme right.

When the first car arrived in Binbrook in 1909 it caused quite a stir. As can be seen from the group who greeted the driver (Mr Lunt from Birmingham), it was a momentous occasion.

Eventually, in about 1913, the Clarkes bought their own Model T Ford. It was photographed in the yard of Binbrook Manor. These new-fangled automobiles would threaten those old shire horses that had faithfully ploughed the land for centuries.

Peter Barton, the Binbrook Manor groom,
photographed in 1914.

In those heady days of 1913 just before the First World War there was time for a football match. It was a
scratch team from Kirmond-le-Mire versus Binbrook with, from left to right, H.W. Clarke, W.J. Clarke,
A. Keller, J. Fieldsend, the Revd Mr Smith, Dr Wilkinson, H. Odling, Parsons Wright, C. Fieldsend, Tod
Wilkinson, Martin Cust, the Revd Mr Bettison (from Wold Newton) and Tom Haxby.

Binbrook had always had strong connections with the RAF. Here we see an FE2.6 flying over Binbrook in 1917.

A close-up of the bi-plane.

When Lieutenant Noel Parker Dixon (from Christchurch, New Zealand) of the Royal Flying Corps (as it was then) married Miss Dorothy Andrews, daughter of the Revd W. Andrews of Claxby Rectory, in Binbrook parish church, there was considerable local interest. Mr Andrews had been rector of Kelstern for a number of years.

Binbrook Manor was used as a recuperation centre for service personnel. Here we see N.P. 'Dickie' Dixon, Dorothy Dixon, N. Garstin, Mrs Clarke, Geoffrey Bone and Norah Wilkinson. All the men are smoking.

Flyers in particular were always welcome. This was Wing Commander Geoffrey Stephenson who was later killed in America.

There was time for tennis as this group shot shows. In the centre of the photograph is Tim Player, of the Nottingham family firm of John Players tobacco.

Ravendale Hall was built in 1720 as a private family home. For years this house served as a retreat to numerous families, including John Wilson Henry Parkinson, Administrative General of Kenya, who died in Mombasa in 1923. A tablet was erected to him in St Martin's Church, East Ravendale. One of the most notable features of this house was its 'bookroom' or library where tomes lined the walls from floor to ceiling. The Hall has recently been converted into a private nursing home – a fate which many similar houses have had to endure.

Cuxwold Hall was built by Henry Thorold in the middle of the nineteenth century. For many years it was the home of Michael Sleight, whose family amassed a fortune from the fishing industry.

This is a sight that was once only too familiar but which has now gone forever – fighter planes at Binbrook. This photograph was taken on Binbrook's twenty-first anniversary. Since its closure in 1982, the airfield at RAF Binbrook has been used in the making of David Puttnam's film *Memphis Belle*, and its quarters have been sold off as private residences.

These days you are more likely to see a hay loader than an aeroplane on any one of the disused airfields dotted about the county.

On the western spur of the Wolds lies the old Roman town of Caistor. This was the Market Place at the turn of the twentieth century.

Even in the fifties this view of the Market Place shows how little Caistor has changed.

One of the oldest houses, built in 1692, shows that Caistor used to be quite an important centre but, as Jack Yates recorded in his *Shell Guide to Lincolnshire*, 'there never seems to be much shopping going on in Caistor and the market square has a depressed aspect.' It is difficult to believe that another poet, Henry Newbolt, attended Caistor Grammar School back in 1873. Sir Henry Newbolt, famous for his 'Play up, play up and play the game', was sent to Caistor Grammar at the age of ten (his father having died in 1866 when Henry Newbolt was four). Anthony Bower, the headmaster of Caistor Grammar, had been his father's old Cambridge tutor and achieved an excellent record of scholarships to Eton and Clifton. In 1878 Henry Newbolt passed his scholarship exam and went to Clifton College, Bristol, where he attended as a day-boy in North Town while his mother lived just around the corner in Worcester Crescent, Clifton. Newbolt's schooling in Lincolnshire has often been overlooked in comparison to that other Victorian denizen, Alfred Lord Tennyson.

Even those travellers who pass through Caistor on their way to Brigg cannot fail to be impressed by some examples of the town's Georgian architecture.

During the Second World War recruits from Caistor readily joined the Home Guard. This photograph was taken in the Rothwell area in about 1943.

Because of the way that Caistor is situated on the side of the Wolds, not only does it have some splendid views but it also makes an excellent toboggan run for children in winter.

Two miles away from Caistor lies Pelham's Pillar, which commemorates the planting of twelve million trees by the first Lord Yarburgh (Charles Anderson Pelham).

It would be very remiss of me to complete a book on the Lincolnshire Wolds and not include a photograph of Brocklesby Hall. This Queen Anne house, which was pruned to its present size after the great fire of 1898, is the home of the Earl of Yarborough. Any man who has enough influence to move the borders of a county, as the present Earl's father did when the short-lived County of Humberside came into force, to include the Brocklesby estate in Lincolnshire rather than Humberside, cannot be excluded.

A typical view of harvesting on the Wolds. Those rolling hills serving as a backcloth make a memorable picture.

Some of the scenery that can be found on the Lincolnshire Wolds is undatable. Take, for example, this view of the Caistor Wolds (*above*) and it is clear that this image would not have changed in the last hundred years or Tealby Thorpe Ford (*below*) with its evocative charm as a shire horse comes into view.

The idyllic journey through the Wolds is continued at Wolds farm, where hay is bound with old fashioned baling twine and stacked along the side of the road.

As opposed to modern combine harvesting where bales of corn are gathered up with almost military precision.

Wherever one looks on the Lincolnshire Wolds there are delightful, almost secret places. From the tiny village of Cuxwold set in a hollow . . .

. . . to the pretty village of Ruckland which is on the road to Tetford. In black and white this photograph echoes shades of the 1960s.

One of the few working mills left in Lincolnshire at Burgh-le-Marsh, only a short distance from Skegness.

Lincolnshire once had many thatched cottages. A typical example is Woodbine Cottage in the centre of South Willingham, situated close to the church of St Martin. It can be seen here on the left of the path. Once part of the Hainton estate, this old stone and thatched cottage (sometimes called 'mud and stud') was sold in 1957 for £70! Formerly a post office and possibly an old bakery, it is now a private residence and one of the few remaining thatched houses on the Lincolnshire Wolds.

ACKNOWLEDGEMENTS

In compiling this book I would like to thank the late James Baildom, Tom Barton, Steven Clarke, Bernard Hallgath, Paul Matthews, Mrs McConnell, John Nielsen and the Welhome Galleries for lending me certain photographs. Once again a special thank you must go to the *Grimsby Evening Telegraph* team of Peter Moore, Peter Craig, Peter Chapman and Janet Longden, without whose help this volume would have been very limp, also to Geoffrey Hardyman and Dr Nicholas Bennett for information, and last, but not least, to Louth Secretarial Services for typing the manuscript so carefully.